Beautiful America's

OREGON

Front cover: Snow-covered Mount Hood from Lost lake

Historic Sumpter Valley Railroad in Baker County

Published by
Beautiful America Publishing Company
P.O. Box 244
Woodburn, OR 97071

Library of Congress Cataloging-in-Publication Data
Library of Congress Catalog Number 2001043419

ISBN 0-89802-745-4
ISBN 0-89802-744-6 (paperback)

Beautiful America's

OREGON

Text by Linda Stirling
Photography by Larry Geddis

Beautiful America Publishing Company

DEDICATION

For Joe

My love, as always, to Keith, Kevin,
Kari, Audra, Jordan, Dillon and Kole.

Thanks, as always, to Beverly and Ted.

OREGON

Hearts were full of dreams when settlers first crossed the border into Oregon. Many pioneers gave all they had materially and physically to plunge ahead into a new land of hope and vision. They found unsurpassed beauty and promise. That same beauty and promise summarize the state today. It is no longer only a land of dreams, but, for many, of dreams come true.

The word-pictures that early explorers painted of Oregon inspired the largest voluntary land migration in history – up to a half million immigrants left what was often a life of comfort to travel 2000 miles in search of new opportunities. Along the way, those mental images of bountiful wildlife, rich soils and waters teeming with fish gave strength to weary immigrants. They envisioned an incredibly diverse land, and their hopes were fulfilled.

Despite the dominant stories of wagon trains that were twenty or thirty wagons long, it was much more common for only two or three wagons to band together. Disputes over whether or not to travel on Sunday or ideas of who should make final decisions for the group winnowed bigger groups down. The wagons that ultimately traveled together were usually the wagons of a few related families. Although encouraged by the government in the early 1840's to travel in groups for protection, these small groups felt comfortable traveling together. In fact, there was little need to form large caravans, since dangerous encounters with Indians were uncommon. More common were sickness, fatigue, and hard work. The Indians who did approach the trains usually came to trade or to ask to be paid for the use of their grazing areas. Sometimes the encounters were tense, but the majority of times the interactions were positive. Once the emigrants arrived, there was an overwhelming amount of work to be done in finding a location for their homes, building their homes, and building their lives in a new land. Because the government had not made treaties with the Indians, several decades of conflicts and battles occurred. When the Civil War broke out, Oregon's remoteness from the rest of the country forced

Imnaha River Canyon, Wallowa County

Opposite: Winter in the Wallowa Mountains

them to become even more independent.

And they were already an independent and stubborn lot. A typical family was that of Jon Baker, first cousin to General Robert E. Lee. Baker's family owned a large tobacco plantation in Wheeling, West Virginia, but as he was not the oldest son there was no inheritance in line for him. His best chances, he believed, lay in the West. He married fifteen-year-old Nancy Haley and in the spring of 1847 the couple and their three children joined a wagon train and set off to make their fortune. Nancy had packed her most treasured possession, the Haley family china, in a large oak cask filled with straw to cushion the china on their journey. Upon reaching a waterless stretch on the eastern side of the Oregon Trail, all the emigrants began to toss everything they could out of the wagons to spare their weary animals. Jon Baker took Nancy's china off the wagon, but Nancy fought to save her treasure. "If this barrel is to remain here in this godforsaken plot of wasteland, then I remain as well," she said. Jon gave in to his wife – and their descendants enjoy the heirlooms to this day.

Modern-day explorers can follow in historic footsteps in comfort. One begins at the state's eastern border and can follow the Oregon Trail to its official end in Oregon City. Self-guided tour maps are available from Oregon's State Tourism Division. The maps detail forty-three historic and scenic points of interest made notable by the 1843 migration.

Eastern Oregon takes up about half the state's geography, but holds only about five percent of the state's population. Crossing this part of Oregon with its wide-open spaces it's easy to visualize the hardships the pioneers endured.

A good starting point for a modern-day trip would be Ontario, Oregon. There, the focus of the Four Rivers Cultural Center is not pioneer days, nevertheless it provides a wonderful history of later settlers, examining the history, heritage and cultures of the Basque sheepherders, European cattlemen, Northern Paiute Indians, Japanese farmers, and Mexican farm workers who worked and settled in the area.

Where Ontario nudges against the Oregon-Idaho border, you can leave the I-84 freeway and follow Highway 201 to the site where wagon trains crossed the Snake River just south of Nyssa.

Here, you may follow the Oregon Trail signs along county roads to Keeney Pass. Deep wagon ruts remain along the route to the Malheur River. Following the route to Vale, you'll find the historic Stone House. Built in 1872, it served as a hotel, store, and post office. Farewell Bend State Park, bordered by the Snake River, was the last stop for the wagon trains before the dreaded Burnt River Canyon. Across the river from Farewell Bend is an area known to locals as The Sand Dunes. Over the decades shifting sands have revealed arrowheads and burial sites of the Indians who crossed the river from Idaho into Oregon and used the same trails as the pioneers.

The next stop in Eastern Oregon for modern travelers is Baker City. The jewel of Baker has to be the Geiser Grand Hotel. This stunning historic landmark was touted as the finest hotel between Salt Lake City and Seattle. Built during the Gold Rush the stained-glass ceiling and mahogany millwork retain the richness they portrayed when built in 1889. An award-winning restaurant is open to guests and delights such as musicians, historic menu recreations, and live dinner theatre may be enjoyed. Another attraction in Baker City is the Adler House Museum. A local philanthropist, Leo Adler, bequeathed his $20 million fortune to Baker County. The Adler House Museum, built in 1889, contains the original Victorian furnishings the Adler family used between 1899 and 1915. The Oregon Trail Regional Museum, another fine Baker City museum, holds artifacts and displays of items that date back to the 1840's. For the best look at the pioneer experience, the Bureau of Land Management's National Historic Oregon Trail Interpretive Center, is the place to visit. When you cash your travelers' checks, stop at the U.S. Bank in Baker City where you can also take a peek at the largest Oregon collection of gold nuggets. The centerpiece is the Armstrong Nugget, weighing in at a whopping 80.4 ounces. Seeing this collection may give you an itch to find some gold of your own. Just 33 miles from Baker City is the Cracker Creek Mining Camp in Sumpter, Oregon. The folks there will teach you the basics of gold mining and let you keep your findings. For the kids in your party that don't think they'll get rich panning for gold, there is a big swimming and fishing hole.

A very different experience can be had in nearby North Powder. Oregon's only horse-drawn Elk Viewing Excursions offers a 30-minute narrated wagon ride that takes viewers within

Eagle Cap Mountain from Sunshine Lake, Eagle Cap Wilderness

Hells Canyon, the deepest gorge in North America

touching distance of 150 –200 head of Rocky Mountain Elk.

Although few pioneers settled in Hells Canyon, there were some who called it home. Only ninety-five miles from Baker City, the fabled canyon offers much to see and do. The 652,488-acre Hells Canyon National Recreation Area was designated by an act of Congress in 1975. Hells Canyon is the deepest river gorge in North America. The designated wilderness area of the canyon is comprised of over 215,000 acres. The Hells Canyon National Recreation Area has fifteen campgrounds. One, the Imnaha River Camp, is adjacent to the Imnaha River, a designated Wild and Scenic River. The Imnaha is critical habitat for the Chinook Salmon and the Bull Trout. It's recommended that you check out campgrounds and find out what each is like, for many are quite primitive. Make sure there's space, too, for it's a long, dark drive to the closest towns and lodging in summertime can get sparse.

The Hells Canyon Creek Recreation Site has access for floaters and jet boaters who want to enjoy this part of the Snake River. Facilities at the site include a small video theatre, interpretive displays, and picnic tables. Up river, the Kirkwood Historical Ranch is the former home of Idaho's Governor Len Jordan. The site has archaeological evidence of human habitation from 7,100 years ago. The site is only reachable by boat or trail. It is staffed by trained volunteers.

The Oregon portion of the Hells Canyon National Recreation Area trail system has 600 miles of trails. Many trails are steep; some line vertical cliffs that drop several hundred feet into the canyon. Most of the trails are difficult and are definitely not for anyone less than a sure-footed, experienced explorer. If boating is more your style, Hells Canyon Adventures conducts guided jet boat tours and whitewater rafting excursions on the Snake. These tours provide a chance to see pictographs, visit ancient caves and explore pioneer homesites.

Rugged and beautiful scenery abounds in this part of the state. If you're in Eastern Oregon, you must see Wallowa County. Wallowa County has 53 lakes that cover 2,449 acres. If that isn't enough, there are 3,100 streams that cover 5,600 miles. The Native American name Wallowa means "Land of Winding Waters." The natural beauty here has inspired and attracted many artists and craftspeople. There are three bronze foundries in the county and a unique art community in the frontier town of Joseph. Valley Bronze of Oregon creates some of the most beautiful artwork to be seen, not only in Oregon, but in the world. This foundry operates two galleries where works by some of their artists may be seen.

Wallowa County has been called the "Switzerland of America." One way to enhance that feeling even further is to take the steepest gondola ride in the U.S. There are plenty of other activities, too. There's fishing and boating, swimming, water skiing, hiking (llamas are an option!), camping, backpacking, horseback riding, pack trips, snowmobiling and much, much more. You might want to be in Enterprise in early August for the historic barn tour. Of course if you do that, you'll have to see the Sunrise Iron Historic Tractor Show.

Before climbing the Blue Mountains, the emigrants that followed the Oregon Trail passed through the fertile Grand Ronde Valley. Today's town, La Grande, dubbed the Valley of Peace by the Indians, sits in a pretty valley surrounded by national forest, lakes and rivers. Site-seeing close to La Grande includes attractions such as the historic Elgin Opera House, the Union County Museum, the Tamastslikt Cultural Institute, and the Wild Horse Gaming Center. With La Grande as a hub, day drives include vistas of the Painted Hills at John Day Fossil Beds National Monument or the 50-mile long fault-block ridge of Steens Mountain, near Burns. The Steens Mountain Fault is the largest geological fault in North America. The Painted Hills are especially colorful after a rainstorm or at dawn and dusk, when color changes are magnified. They display many unusual colors due to the weathering of volcanic ash that was deposited up to forty million years ago. The glacier-eroded gorge 4,100 feet beneath Steens Mountain, Alvord Basin, is filled with wildflowers in the spring and early summer. Near Burns and Hines, off Highway 78, lie a number of historic sites, including Crystal Crane Hot Springs and the thunder egg fields along Buchanan Road. South of Burns and Hines, Highway 205 leads to Wright's Point and Sunset Valley, fine hunting grounds for agate hunting. The highway divides massive Malheur and Harney Lakes, known for their waterfowl. Along this route you may spot golden eagles flying above you and wild mustangs roaming the land. Hart Mountain is home to antelope, deer and California bighorn sheep. Off Highway 395 lies Lakeview, known as the Hang Gliding Capital of

The Painted Hills amid yellow bee wildflowers

Cathedral Rock, John Day Fossil Beds National Monument

the West. It is also home to Hunter's Hot Springs Geyser. This area, Lake County, has plenty of recreational opportunities, including rock hounding for sunstones and thunder eggs, and fishing and camping at Lake Abert, Summer Lake and Goose Lake.

The John Day Fossil Loop is a full-day trip of great variety. If you start on Highway 26, in the heart of Oregon's gold and cattle country, where gold worth more than $26 million was mined before the end of the Gold Rush, you can see the Kam Wah Chung and Co. Museum in John Day. Follow the John Day River west on Highway 26 and you'll discover dramatic Picture Gorge, which gets its name from the Native American pictographs on its walls. You'll also see the multicolored ash beds of the John Day Fossil Beds that rise nearly 2,000 feet. These beds are the richest find of prehistoric fossils in the world. From Highway 19 follow the John Day River past Goose Rock Conglomerate, a 110-million-year-old formation. North of the highway, camel and pronghorn fossils have been found. At Service Creek, don't miss a side trip to Fossil where you can dig in an open fossil bed for plant and insect fossils over 30 million years old. Twenty miles west of Fossil on Highway 218 are dramatic palisades with many preserved fossils in the tall mudstone spires. If you get your fill of driving these scenic loops, settle back in at La Grande. Because the town is home to Eastern Oregon University, a level of culture and entertainment is found that usually isn't seen in small communities.

To keep close to the Trail, follow I-84 through the steep and beautiful Blue Mountains (your trip will be much faster than that of the pioneers). You'll gasp for breath over the descent from the Blues that drops you into the town of Pendleton. Once you've reached Pendleton, you have traveled almost half way across the upper part of the state. The Underground Tours give you a lively look at Pendleton's infamous and entertaining past. Your underground guide will take you through the Shamrock Card Room, Hop Sing's Chinese Laundry, the Empire Ice Cream Company, a 1920's Prohibition Card Room, the Cozy Room Bordello, and Chinese living quarters. A 90-minute tour runs year-round.

The highway outside Pendleton diverges from the Oregon Trail, but parallels its course. From I-84 you can take Highway 207/74 through Ione and Arlington to see the historical sites at Well

Steens Mountain and glacier-formed Wildhorse Lake

Springs and Four Mile Canyon. Here, a favorite part of the Trail begins for modern travelers, for this is the beginning of the Columbia River Gorge, one of the most beautiful places in the world.

Today's travelers can find that same diverse land the pioneers traveled, with much of its riches preserved. There is an undeniable breath of history and legend that permeates the Columbia River Gorge creating an almost visible presence. This presence floats among the shreds of mist off Bridal Veil Falls; it is in a petroglyph embedded in the sheer walls of a basalt cliff; in a spirit howling round the canyon when the wind blows at midnight. The Gorge remains one of the most majestic areas in the world. With the Cascade Mountains rearing craggy heights of up to 4,000 feet on each side of the river, the Columbia surges through the great cliffs, creating the only sea-level break through the Cascade Range to the Pacific Ocean. Adding to the visual feast are nearly 75 waterfalls; hundreds of hiking trails for novices to experts; trees and wildflowers that are found, in some cases, only in this part of the world; and birds and animals of many species. When your sensations or your trekking legs are overloaded, there are always the towns to visit, with their variety of attractions; the lazy lure of fishing under bright skies; or, for the spunky, the more contemporary thrills of windsurfing.

At The Dalles emigrants had to choose between rafting down the Columbia (which didn't have the dams it has today, so the river wasn't the placid, slow moving river seen on your drive), or they took the rugged Barlow Road route that circled around Mt. Hood. Lewis and Clark visited The Dalles twice. Their Rock Fort campsite stands at the water's edge near the center of town. Throughout the town murals reflect the history of the area.

The pleasant city of The Dalles was named by French canoemen who were employed by early fur traders. Dalle means flagstone, which was often used to flag gutters, and the rocky chute the canoeists had to master reminded them of a gutter. History buffs can take a look at the Fort Dalles Surgeon's Quarters, which was a strategic military post in the mid 1800's and now houses the Fort Dalles Museum. Be sure to allow time to watch sailboarders from around the world sail among the world-famous winds and waves that churn the waters of the Columbia River into a windsurfer's dream. Watching the bright sailboards is like watching a flock of brilliant-colored parrots diving and swooping over a crystal blue lake.

If you time your trip right, the small site of Celilo Village, nearby, is the home to Native American's powwows each spring and fall.

Just east of The Dalles, Highway 197 mirrors The Barlow Road. You can take this circle, passing through Tygh Valley, Wamic and around Mt. Hood. This passage was forged in 1845 by Samuel Barlow and Joel Palmer. Ruts left by the pioneers' wagons are still visible near the Sandy River. In Sandy, Jonsrud Viewpoint overlooks the terrain of The Barlow Road from Mt. Hood to Sandy.

Mt. Hood, the tallest of Oregon's Cascade peaks, stands guard over this part of Oregon. The glacier-laden peak, rising to 11,239 ft., is home to year-round skiing and snowboarding, offering the longest season in North America. Mid-way to the summit of Mt. Hood is Timberline Lodge. It is a masterpiece of architecture, constructed of mammoth timbers. The lodge has an ambiance of warmth and friendliness, definitely a great spot to spend a few days. A stay could include trips to any of the five major ski areas, the alpine slide, or a visit to the Wasson Winery for a sip of award-winning raspberry wine.

If you travel back to The Dalles, another interesting stop is The Dalles Dam, built in the 1950's. Tourists can hop on the small train and take a tour of the dam. You can see Indian art preserved in the cliff sides here. If you look closely as you travel near the river, you will also be able to see Indian fishing platforms where each season thousands of salmon were netted or speared and brought to shore.

Ten miles east of the dam you'll find Celilo Park, a monument to Celilo Falls. Celilo Falls was a favorite fishing place for Indians, and a churning spigot of water that generally had to be portaged by traders and trappers. The falls disappeared forever under the backwaters of The Dalles Dam. The little park makes a lovely stopping spot for highway travelers.

Further along I-84, at the base of the Hood River Valley lies the town of Hood River, known as the "sailboarding capital of the world." It is a town long synonymous in the minds of Oregonians with apples, pears, and cherries. Produce from the prolific Hood River Valley is shipped all over the world. Like The Dalles, Hood River is praised by the windsurfing crowd. One of the most

Oregon Trail ruts at Biggs Plateau, Sherman County

Opposite: Oregon's tallest peak, beautiful Mount Hood (11,235 ft)

popular sailing sites in The Gorge is the sailpark at the Hood River Port Marina Park. World windsurfing competitions are often held there.

Take some time to explore this charming area of Oregon. Consider a ride on the Historic Mt. Hood Railroad. Since 1906 the railroad served as a lifeline for the Hood River Valley, delivering the region's famous pears, peaches, cherries, apricots, apples and wood products to the markets in Portland. This railroad features old-style cars and provides riders with scenic trips through the Hood River Valley. The train still keeps to the tradition of picking up cars of fruit and lumber.

The Hood River Museum gives visitors a chance to learn about Indians, explorers, pioneers, native plants, the fruit and timber industry, mountain climbing and more. The Hood River Visitors Center helps flesh out knowledge of the local area.

Downtown Hood River holds interesting shops and historic buildings. The city traces its formal history back to its platting in 1881.

Scenic car routes from Hood River could include a country road trip to Lost Lake. Twenty-five miles south of Hood River is one of the most photographed lakes in the nation. Lost Lake has it all: terrific scenery, hiking trails, camping, cabins, fishing, rowboats, and a small store.

Before leaving the Hood River area, take Highway 35 along the east edge of the town then follow the signs to Panorama Point. Here, the mountains and the Hood River Valley can be seen from atop a small pinnacle. It's a breathtaking view, enhanced even more if enjoyed during the springtime when the valley explodes with fruit blossoms.

One of the loveliest spots to relax is the Columbia River Gorge Hotel. This magnificent old hotel enjoys a worldwide reputation. Built in 1921, it was the brainchild of millionaire Simon Benson. Perhaps even more beautiful today than when built, the hotel perches on a cliff, high above the river. Stunningly manicured park-like grounds surround the hotel and four-star Wah-Gwin-Gwin Falls tumbles over boulders behind the hotel before dropping from sight. Since each room was unique, the service superb, and the quality of meals renowned, the Columbia River Gorge Hotel drew people from all over the world. The hotel remains a gentle, graceful place, and fortunately, its continued fame has not caused it to be overpriced. Even those who are not movie stars or political royalty can afford to enjoy the pleasures of a room restored to its 1920 grandeur.

And then there is the great highway Lancaster built – great in the sense it was built with the preservation of scenery being a primary objective, great too in the sense it was a miracle of construction for a time when only mule power and the energy of men fueled its development. Panoramic views, picnic spots, and access to waterfall viewing were as much a consideration as whether automobiles could race from one side of the state to the other.

Much of the scenic Columbia Gorge Highway can no longer be traveled. Traveling west, take the Dodson or Warrendale exit. Other access is by taking Interstate 84 exits at either Troutdale, Lewis and Clark State Park, Corbett, or Bridal Veil.

One of the most wonderful provisions of the Scenic Highway is the access provided to waterfalls. The Multnomah Falls area is the best known since it can be seen in part from Interstate 84. All falls in this area are accessible from the Columbia Gorge Scenic Highway and there is access to many from the Multnomah Falls Rest Area (exit 31) off Interstate 84. Falls in this area include Mist Falls, Wahkeena Falls, Necktie Falls, Fairy Falls, Multnomah Falls, Dutchman Falls, and Double Falls.

Multnomah Falls is the fourth highest waterfall in the United States. The main fall plunges 542 feet and Lower Multnomah Falls drops an additional 69 feet, with the total drop between the two falls coming to 620 feet. There's a trail to the top and at the 1¼-mile mark, a side trail leads to a viewpoint over Multnomah Falls. Further up the mountain lies Little Multnomah Falls, which has a descent of only ten to fifteen feet. It's worth the trek for the view.

Atop the Scenic Highway lies Crown Point State Park, a designated National Natural Landmark. Crown Point is the remains of a 25-million-year-old basalt flow. It is believed the flow completely filled the canyon but all except this promontory were swept away in the great floods that came through. Rooster Rock, on the canyon floor, is a portion that broke off and slid down. The unusual structure of Crown Point Vista House was built as a memorial to the pioneers. Inside the castle-like fortress you can buy snacks or gifts, as well as learn more about the area's history.

Sunrise at Timberline Lodge (1935) on Mount Hood

Windsurfer's paradise, the Columbia River Gorge

The Sternwheeler Columbia Gorge *at Cascade Locks*

Operated by Friends of Vista House, in cooperation with Oregon State Parks, the facility is open April 15th through October 15th.

Rooster Rock State Park was once the site of a salmon cannery. Rooster Rock has attained popularity equal to that of Oregon's ocean beaches because of its long bathing beach which has a wide strip of shallow water for young people to enjoy. The park can be reached from Interstate 84.

Turn off at Eagle Creek Park if you're interested in a refreshing hike that can provide unparalleled scenery. The trail takes you past several waterfalls within the Eagle Creek Drainage. There are eight falls along Eagle Creek Trail. The largest and most stunning are Metlako Falls and Punch Bowl Falls. Metlako was named in 1915 for the legendary Indian Goddess of the salmon by a committee of the Mazamas, an outdoor climbing and recreation group. Punchbowl Falls is a smaller fall in comparison to many of the others in the Gorge, but rates up there as one of the prettiest. The descent of the falls is short, only about fifteen feet, but the pool formed beneath lies within the realm of fairytales. Few would argue that Eagle Creek Trail is one of the most popular and gorgeous hiking trails in the Pacific Northwest. Traveling any of the hundreds of fern-laden paths causes one to reflect upon earlier times and the effect of the land upon the people who lived here.

The next significant stop downriver is the Bridge of the Gods. A magnificent structure, it is cited in the National Register of Historic Places. Nearby picnic spots make appropriate stopping places.

Cascade Locks, the little town that leads to the Bridge of the Gods just off Interstate 84, is an historic little community where the locks are now designated as a National Historic Site. Visitors will find a park, a marina, and a museum. The Cascade Locks Historical Museum, located in the Cascade Locks Port Marine Park, makes for an interesting stop. On display is the first steam train built on the Pacific Coast, the Oregon Pony. The remains of the original locks through the cascades are nearby. Cascade Locks Marina Park is a stop-off in June through October for the Columbia Gorge Sternwheeler, an authentic reproduction of an old-time riverboat. The Cascade Queen also does tours. The Queen of West has its own jazz band and seventy-three richly-furnished staterooms. Sternwheeler cruises are offered daily during the summer season, and there are a variety of dinner cruises and special voyages.

At the west end of the Colombia River Scenic Highway, you will find the city of Troutdale. At the base of the cliff that houses the historic district lies a popular outlet mall. Overlooking the outlet stores is a single street of the most charming shops and art galleries. The Harlow House Museum, built in 1900, provides a good history lesson.

The city of Troutdale edges the fertile Willamette Valley, a rich green valley that was truly the pioneers' promised land. The valley takes its name from the river that flows through it, and it's perhaps known best for the richness of land, a producer of all kinds of fruits, vegetables, herbs, nuts, flowers, and trees. The Willamette Valley is home, also, to the state capital, Salem, and to its largest city, Portland.

Portland, the City of Roses, is worthy of several days stay, for travelers have much to savor. Even long-time inhabitants have rarely seen it all. Its diverse offerings have something for everyone. Portland straddles the Willamette River and is bordered by the Columbia River on the northern edge. Mount Hood and Mount Saint Helens are snow-capped volcanoes that rise in the skyline. In the city, parks abound and stunning private gardens are the norm. Over 7,500 acres of parks in 160 locations are open to the public. Parks range from the smallest park in the world to the largest urban wilderness in any American city.

The Tom McCall Waterfront Park is a two-mile greenway that showcases many summer activities and offers a chance to relax in the middle of the city. Tucked above the city are three nationally acclaimed gardens; the Japanese Garden, featuring five formal garden styles on 5.5 acres in Portland's Washington Park; the International Rose Test Garden, with more than 500 varieties of roses; and Hoyt Arboretum. All of these fabulous gardens are worthy of a day's exploration. New to Portland is the Classical Chinese Garden in downtown Portland. Called Lan Su Yuan, or "Garden of the Awakening Orchid," this garden showcases several hundred plants from Portland's sister city of Suzhou, China. The garden was built as a partnership between Portland and Suzhou to celebrate more than 500 years of horticulture in China's garden city as well as the numerous connections among Portland's diverse Asian communities. Eighty Suzhou

The historic, charming Columbia Gorge Hotel at Hood River

Oregon's tallest waterfall, beautiful Multnomah Falls (611 ft)

craftsmen in China shaped every tile, stone and beam in the garden and then traveled to Portland and assembled the buildings and garden structure.

During the month of June, Portland puts on its party hat for the Rose Festival. In addition to the fabulous parade, that rivals the famous Pasadena Rose Bowl Parade, there are dozens of activities to choose from each week, including carnival rides, airshows, car races, and more.

Any time of year there is much to consider for a choice of activities in Portland. Consider a visit to the Oregon Museum of Science and Industry where you can feel the power of an earthquake, experience a real submarine, or explore the globe in a five-story high domed theatre. There are over 200 interactive exhibits. Cultural Portland might include the Portland Art Museum and the Portland Center for the Performing Arts. On most Saturdays and Sundays throughout the year the Portland Saturday Market, held under the Burnside Bridge in downtown Portland, will offer a huge selection of hand-crafted made-in-Oregon artwork and other crafts.

The twin spires of the Oregon Convention Center mark a Portland landmark for events. The Center provides over a half-million square feet of meeting rooms and convention space. Only Portland can so gracefully combine business and beauty.

If there's one business not to miss in Portland, it has to be Powell's City of Books, the largest new and used bookstore in the world. It occupies an entire city block of Portland and stocks more than a million new and used books. Nine color-coded rooms house over 3,500 different sections, including an incredible selection of out-of-print and hard-to-find titles. The Rare Book Room gathers autographed first editions and other collectible volumes.

From Portland, it's a tough call whether to travel first to the Oregon Coast, or to start exploration of the remainder of the Willamette Valley. Since the major highways of Northwest Oregon all come together in Portland, one can pick any direction without difficulty.

If you choose to leave Portland and head slightly southwest to Highway 99W, you are in for a pleasant tour of some of the most beautiful wine country in the United States. You will find cities like Newberg, Dundee and McMinnville absolutely charming. One new attraction just outside McMinnville on the loop Highway 18, is drawing raves and record crowds. It is the Evergreen

Aviation Museum, right across the highway from the McMinnville Airport, the new home of the famous Howard Hughes wooden flying boat, the "Spruce Goose." For the airplane fancier it is a wonderful trip back into aviation history, with a stunning display of vintage aircraft. Their mission statement, "To inspire and educate, to promote and preserve aviation history, and to honor the patriotic service of our veterans," makes this an attraction you don't want to miss.

If you head south along I-5, you will get a great glimpse of the agricultural wealth of this fertile land. There are hundreds of commercial nurseries and world-acclaimed gardens. Schreiner's Iris Gardens, for example, has hundreds of acres of magnificent iris to see. Schreiner's is the nation's largest retail grower of iris. Their catalog best describes their offerings: "from the deepest black to pure white, fire red to azure blue, glowing copper to velvety purple. Solid color blooms contrast with multi-hued beauties." Ten beautifully designed viewing acres are open, at no charge, to the public. Other off-the-road stops should include Heirloom Roses, Adelman Peony Gardens, Wooden Shoe Bulb Company, Cooley's Iris Gardens, and a delightful nursery with a wonderful display garden, Ferguson's Fragrant Gardens.

Nearby, a stunning spot for a picnic and exploring is Silver Falls State Park. There are ten magnificent waterfalls to hike around – and even behind. The variety of walking trails provides scenic delights.

The newest horticultural achievement in Oregon is the Oregon Garden. To quote their mission statement, "The Oregon Garden will be a botanically challenging, world-class facility which will showcase the wealth and diversity of plant material in a visually compelling manner. It will be a landscaped approach to plant display, resulting in a garden that is a skillfully arranged environmental laboratory for education, research and public enjoyment." The goals are well underway, with sixty acres of the ultimate 240 acres already open to the public. They've thought of everything to make your visit great, even daycare for your pets while you take in the garden! Just forty miles south of Portland, it is a must stop!

The city of Salem, like Portland, offers much for the modern traveler to enjoy. Younger travelers will have a great treat if you give them the chance to see the National Toy Hall of Fame

A spectacular view of Crown Point, Vista House and the Columbia River Gorge

and A.C. Gilbert's Discovery Village. Built by native Oregonian A.C. Gilbert, the inventor of Erector Sets and Gilbert Chemistry Sets, the Village is a private nonprofit children's museum located in downtown Salem's Riverfront Park. A.C. Gilbert graduated from Yale with a medical degree, earned an Olympic medal in the pole vault, and went on to market not only the Erector Set, but a variety of other educational toys ranging from American Flyer trains to Mysto Magic sets, chemistry and telegraph sets.

The fun and challenging exhibits in the Discovery Village are designed to stimulate educational experiences and spark children's natural curiosity. The Gilbert House, which now houses the museum, was built in 1887 and is a Queen Ann Victorian of Eastlake design that is on the National Register of Historic Places. The Josiah L. Parrish House (circa 1860) houses the National Toy Hall of Fame, and the Rockenfield House (1883), the Little Gem Grocery (1925) and the Wilson-Durbin House (1861) are all used as part of the Discovery Village operation. In the "backyard" is the largest community-built project in Salem's history—the finest outdoor children's discovery center in the Northwest. In nineteen days, 6,000 volunteers and 346 businesses used over twenty miles of lumber and two tons of nails and fasteners to create a 22,000-square foot outdoor facility. Here, children can climb the world's largest Erector Set tower, play on the musical ensemble deck, captain the Paddle Wheeler, watch drama performances, or explore the inside of an animal cell. Bigger kids (uh, much bigger) don't mind this travel stop much either.

Another project that citizens of Salem banded together to create was the Riverfront Carousel project. The entire project, from the carving of the beautiful horses to the construction of the building that houses the carousel, was done with donatiions and volunteer effort. The project is an amazing testament to community cooperation. In addition to the stunning hand-carved carousel, that delights children of all ages, a huge pipe organ sets the tune, while a well-stocked gift shop attracts others. All this on a spacious green landscape that is perfect for family picnics.

Maybe bridges are your ticket. If so, you'll want to take the Willamette Valley Covered Bridge Loop. Built to protect their wooden platforms from the abundant rainfall of the region, the

The city of Portland with Mount Hood as the backdrop

RiverPlace, Portland's urban resort on the Willamette River

The historic Pittock Mansion (1914) in Pittock Acres Park

bridges also became known as kissing bridges for the shelter they offered couples in search of a bit of privacy. By car or bike, you can tour a dozen of Oregon's remaining covered bridges that are showcased on two loops that surround the Albany and Cottage Grove areas just off I-5. For detailed directions, check Oregon's Linn County Road Department. In all, the Willamette Valley has three dozen covered bridges.

While you're touring this area, keep your eyes open for more than thirty wineries in this part of the Willamette Valley. The fertile and agriculturally abundant valley is famous for its wines, which are ranked among the finest in the world. Oregon grapes ripen gradually, under moderate temperatures. This leisurely ripening is, according to wine experts, key to memorable wines that display their full character. These growing conditions and the clay-loam soils have helped Oregon emerge into a leading wine producer. Oregon now has 175 wineries and over 15,000 acres of wine grapes.

An Oregon trail to consider would be the Cascade Lakes Highway. Eighty-seven miles of highway loop through the Mt. Bachelor area and through the alpine lakes area of Central Oregon. The vistas make this scenic drive one never to be forgotten. This loop is one that's closed from November to May beyond Mt. Bachelor because of snow.

The first stop from Portland would be Bend. This town has grown in the past several years into one of the most desirable places to live in Oregon. Warm summers–would you believe there's sunshine nearly 300 days a year?–and snow-filled winters make it a perfect place for the outdoorsman. Just twenty miles from town, Mt. Bachelor rises above the desert floor. The powder-fine snow brings snowsport enthusiasts from around the world to ski, snowboard, and snowmobile. During the summer the high desert landscape of Central Oregon provides a view of the snowcapped Cascade peaks and the geologic marvels of Smith Rock State Park, Newberry National Volcanic Monument and Lava Lands. Natives and tourists alike enjoy fly-fishing, hiking, rock climbing, biking and golfing in this area. A summer chairlift to the top of Mt. Bachelor will give you a bird's eye view of the beauty. The Inn Of The Seventh Mountain is one of the premier resorts in the area and it expands the recreational opportunities even further. It has jogging and hiking trails, tennis courts, swimming pools, interpretive canoe trips, guided horseback rides, and more. The resort includes two championship gold courses, tennis courts, stables, a resort marina, the Sunriver Nature Center, a botanical garden and a planetarium.

The High Desert Museum in Bend is a star attraction. Founded in 1974, the museum is regarded as one of the best educational and cultural institutions in the western United States. The museum's exhibits and presentations cover the area's history, culture, arts, and wildlife.

Not far from Bend is the Newberry National Volcanic Monument, the West's newest national monument. The massive volcano includes a five-mile wide caldera that offers obsidian fields, deep mountain lakes, lava forests and formations, and waterfalls. The site was popular with Native Americans as a location for obsidian, a material valued in the formation of their tools and weapons. Records of these people go back 10,000 years. During the time they came to the area, the Newberry Volcano was very active. There were explosions of ash and pumice and lava flowed freely. These formed new obsidian sources: the Interlake and Gamehut flows; the East Lake flows; and the Big Obsidian flow. The eruptions that caused each of these flows and the eruption of Mt. Mazama (which created Crater Lake) buried many of the native camps and quarry sites under tons of volcanic ash and debris. These ancient sites are now archaeological sites that can reveal the lives and cultures of the people who lived in those times.

About 6,000 years ago, eruptions sent pahoehoe lava surging to the earth's surface and spilling down the mountains to cover the pine forest. Sap stored in the trees was converted to steam which then cooled the lava and prevented some of the trees from burning completely. These trees were either turned to ash or transformed to charcoal depending on how much oxygen was available to them. Mold formed around the tree trunks, cooling to fashion a hard coat. When the lava slowly receded these molds of trees stood high above the lava surface. This area is known as the Lava Cast Forest. The Newberry Crater has a rich archeological and geological history to study. The crater holds evidence of humans who lived there thousands of years ago. Archaeologists have uncovered several sites of ancient human activity. Using radiocarbon dating, they have determined that some of their findings are 9,000 years old. The site on the

Beautiful fall color at Portland's Japanese Garden

Portland's Classical Chinese Garden, the largest authentic Suzhou-style garden outside China

The classic Oregon State Capitol in Salem

west side of Paulina Lake is one of the most unique in the Northwest, dating to over 8,200 years old. It provides the chance to learn how humans lived and adapted to the volcanic eruptions in that area. Artifacts discovered include spear and dart points that belonged to one of the earliest and least documented cultures in North America.

The Big Obsidian Flow, within Newberry Crater, is the most recent volcanic eruption in Oregon at a young 1,300 years of age. Black volcanic glass was created when rhyolite lava spilled to the valley floor. It has attracted human visitors for thousands of years. Visitors to this area will see evidence of a wider variety of volcanic action in a more compressed area than anywhere else in the United States.

Surrounding Mt. Bachelor is the alpine lake country, dubbed the High-Mountain Playground. Lakes there include the 600-acre Sparks Lake, which was chosen as the memorial site to commemorate the work of Ray Atkeson, Oregon's photographer laureate. There are several roads into the 200,000-acre Three Sisters Wilderness where you can find 111 lakes and miles of trails. Just beyond is Devils Lake which has a white pumice floor; Elk Lake, with a year-round resort; Hosmer Lake, famous for its Atlantic salmon population; Lava and Cultus lakes, both with resorts; and Crane Prairie Reservoir, which is known both for its fishing and for its importance as a breeding ground for osprey. As the highway loops eastward you'll find North and South Twin Lakes and Wickiup Reservoir.

Further south and west is another scenic drive that takes in two outstanding rivers and a national park that's revered all over the world. This drive, about 172-miles, takes in the towns of Ashland, Medford, and Roseburg, skirts the edges of the indigo waters of Crater Lake, Diamond Lake, and the wild Umpqua and Rogue rivers. There are waterfalls, campgrounds and parks and much more to delight you along this drive.

A town that is sure to become a favorite is the charming town of Ashland. Known best as the home of the acclaimed Oregon Shakespeare Festival, the town has a charming atmosphere that will make a stay worthwhile. The Festival is in session in three theatres from mid-February to late October and is known world-wide for the quality of theatrical productions. In the winter, Mt.

Ashland has downhill and cross-country skiing to enjoy. From Ashland take Highway 99 and make a side-trip of the historic 24-mile Jacksonville Route. This route meanders through the Rogue Valley orchards and provides offshoots to several other scenic drives. Jacksonville is host to the Britt Music Festival which offers jazz, pop, country and classical productions from mid-June to Labor Day. The Rogue Valley is home to over a dozen wineries. Since it's also the nation's largest supplier of pears, you might want to time your trip to take this into account.

If you take Highway 238 west to Grants Pass, you'll experience the 40-mile Applegate Valley Tour. The Applegate Trail was the southern route of the Oregon Trail. Blazed in 1846 by three brothers, Lindsay, Jesse, and Charles Applegate, the trail was an attempt at finding an alternate and, hopefully, safer route to Oregon. The brothers lost two sons and an uncle (they drowned when rafting the river) when they came to Oregon on the original Oregon Trail during the 1843 migration, thus they were determined to save others the heartache they experienced. Armed with this desire, they forged a new trail that began in the area today known as Rickreall and traveled down the Willamette Valley through the Corvallis/Eugene area. They continued south of Ashland, then east over Greensprings Mountain, and through Oregon and Nevada before they reached the Humboldt River and turned north along the river for 200 miles. In 1853 alone, over 3,500 men, women and children took the new Applegate Trail. Today, Interstate 5 and Highway 66 travel the same route.

Grants Pass, as a gateway to the Applegate Trail and to the Rogue River, attracts visitors from all over the world. Many activities will interest you in staying for a visit, including rafting, fly fishing, wonderful antique shops, and jet boat excursions.

The official scenic highway of this area begins in Gold Hill where you'll have fun watching gravity do strange things at the Oregon Vortex. Highway 234 leads to wilderness areas and hiking trails. It is also one route into the Rogue River and the Rogue River National Forest. The Rogue Forest area sprawls across central southern Oregon, overflowing slightly into northern California. It encompasses 33,200 acres and ranges in elevation from 2,800 to over 6,700 feet. On the west lies the Applegate River and the Siskiyou Mountains with their narrow canyons and

Salem's Riverfront Carousel

The Oregon Garden in Silverton, a must stop for all visitors

high, steep ridges. On the east lies the upper reaches of the Rogue River, a designated "wild and scenic" river and one of the most dramatic rivers in the United States. White-water enthusiasts are guaranteed an uncrowded, pristine environment. Narrow canyons edged by tall cliffs, old growth Douglas fir, and grass-filled meadows attract abundant wildlife. Beaver, deer, otter, cougars, elk, black bear, osprey, bald eagles, wild turkeys, and ducks abound in the area. Beautiful 90-acre Fish Lake is worth seeing, and there are a number of Rogue River raft trips available with guides and camp or lodge trip options. Trail hiking offers a plethora of day hike options that provide a wonderful perspective of the river and its magnificent scenery.

Highway 138, the Rogue-Umpqua Scenic Byway, is known as the "highway of waterfalls." The Umpqua River is enjoyed for its fishing, kayaking, hiking, whitewater rafting, and camping opportunities. The North Umpqua River is a torrent of whitewater that helmeted kayakers adore. Fishermen can count on a bountiful summer run of steelhead from the river. The Umpqua National Forest is named for the Umpqua Indians, one of several tribes who inhabited the Umpqua drainage in the early nineteenth century. They were deported in mass to the Grand Ronde and Siletz Reservations following the Rogue River Indian wars that broke out in the fall of 1855.

Near the North Umpqua River lies Diamond Lake. At the base of Mt. Thielsen, this lake has a full-service resort. Diamond Lake also boasts of the largest campground in Oregon and Washington and is a popular base camp for exploring the eight wilderness areas that surround the area. Lemolo Lake is another pretty lake nearby. The route passes Toketee Reservoir, the Boulder Creek Wilderness, countless parks and campgrounds, class three and four whitewater challenges, and many trails that lead to scenic waterfalls. During winter months 8,363-foot Mt. Bailey is touted as the best powder-skiing spot in the region.

From Diamond Lake it's just a short drive to Crater Lake National Park. This spectacular lake, the deepest in North America and the seventh deepest in the world, formed when 12,000-foot Mt. Mazama collapsed thousands of years ago. The lake's beauty belies its violent creation. Approximately 7,700 years ago when Mt. Mazama erupted, the volcano collapsed in on itself, forming the large caldera. Lava flows sealed the bottom of the caldera and after time the basin filled with snow and rain. To experience the lake, you could merely take the 33-mile drive around the top of the crater; but there are many scenic, historic trails, or a great two-hour boat ride around the shoreline and to Wizard Island and Phantom Ship Rock is available. A beautiful restored lodge offers summertime accommodations and dining. Winter and its extreme conditions (and winter here is October to June!) provides the kind of conditions that cross-country skiers and snowshoe enthusiasts love. The rim of the lake has some of the best cross-country skiing in the country. There's even a multi-day thirty-three mile circuit, complete with snow camping. There's an average of 533 inches of snowfall in the Crater Lake area each year–that ought to be enough to play in, don't you think?

A tour route that wasn't possible in its present-day form for the pioneers was a tour of the Oregon Coast. While the United States has many beautiful areas, the Oregon Coast is truly special. Whole vacations could easily be focused around one small portion of the coast, for there are so many delightful places to explore and things to do.

For the pioneers the city of Astoria, on the tip of Oregon's northwest coast, was an important destination. Named after John Jacob Astor, it sports the distinction of being the oldest American settlement west of the Rockies. In May of 1792, Captain Robert Gray discovered the Columbia River where it reaches the ocean and he sailed inland as far as Tongue Point. In December 1805, Captains Meriwether Lewis and William Clark completed their expedition from St. Louis and built Fort Clatsop, where they wintered over in preparation for the long trip back. Old Highway 101 takes you right to the Fort Clatsop National Memorial, where the Lewis and Clark Expedition wintered in 1805 through 1806. The fort deteriorated over the years, but in 1955 a replica was built on the site. Nearby, Fort Stevens has more than 600 campsites, including sites for recreational vehicles. Fort Stevens was built during the Civil War. Closed as a military post in 1947, its history has been preserved in a museum as well as in the remaining battery and gun emplacements.

In 1811 John Jacob Astor's men established a fur trading post on the bank of the Columbia River and named it Astoria. Today, Astoria is being rediscovered by tourists who want to take a

South Falls, Silver Falls State Park

Willamette Valley Vineyard in Turner

step back in time. The city itself is composed of Victorian cottages layered on a hill above the wharf and city center, and many of these restored Victorian-style homes are open for tours. The best way to find what's available for viewing is to make the Captain George Flavel Mansion your first stop. Here, you can see the most lovely of homes, plus pick up a map for further touring. Don't miss the beautiful Queen Anne-style home that houses the Clastsop County Historical Society. Astoria is also home to the Columbia River Maritime Museum on Astoria's waterfront. Recognized as one of the finest collections of its kind on the West Coast, the museum preserves the maritime heritage of the Columbia River basin and the north coast area. Outside the museum is the lightship Columbia, the last U.S. Coast Guard lightship to serve on the Pacific Coast.

The Heritage Museum exhibits encompass Native American artifacts, nautical history, early settlement exhibits, logging exhibits, commercial fishing history and artifacts concerning the twenty-two ethnic groups that have lived in Clatsop County. Another great museum in town is the Fire Fighters Museum.

The best-known symbol of Astoria would perhaps be the Astoria Column. Descendants of fur trader John Jacob Astor and the Northern Pacific Railway are responsible for the construction of the column, which was patterned after the Trajan Column erected in Rome by Emperor Trajan in 114 A.D. The monument rises 125 feet to survey the surrounding countryside.

Another attention-getter is the Astoria Bridge. Long popular in television commercials and general photography, the bridge is a stunning piece of architecture. At 4.1 miles across, it has the distinction of being the longest continuous truss span bridge in the world.

South of Astoria lies Seaside, the Pacific Northwest's largest beach resort community. A two-mile promenade of shops, restaurants and arcades offers a glorious feast for both those who love to buy and those who love to window shop. If shopping is less action than you'd like, there are numerous hiking trails in this area. You can choose from designated trails that begin at state parks and make loops back into the forest or meander along the headlands, or trails that merely skirt through the woods or wind near a river or creek.

Of the established trails, four are noted favorites. Saddle Mountain Trail is a one-day hike that

Mount Bachelor (9,065 ft) in the Deschutes National Forest

Spring at the Sara Hite Memorial Rose Garden in Milwaukie

The Swan Island Dahlia Farm of Canby

Mount Washington (7,794 ft) from Big Lake

Central Oregon's dramatic volcanic formation known as Fort Rock

Beautiful Opal Creek in the Opal Creek Wilderness

Oregon's Mount Jefferson (10,495 ft) and Russell Lake

Three Sisters from Scott Lake

Rafters on the Deschutes enjoy the excitement of Big Eddy, a class three rapids

The Wild and Scenic Deschutes River

A spectacular view of the Ochoco Mountains from North Point

The Crooked River and always-popular Smith Rock State Park

Early morning at China Hat and Pruitt's Castle in Malheur County

The beautiful volcanic spires of Leslie Gulch, Malheur County

The Pillars of Rome, Malheur County

Late evening winter light on beautiful Crater Lake National Park

The Wild Cat Covered Bridge of Lane County

The historic Nunan Mansion (1892) of National Historic Landmark, Jacksonville

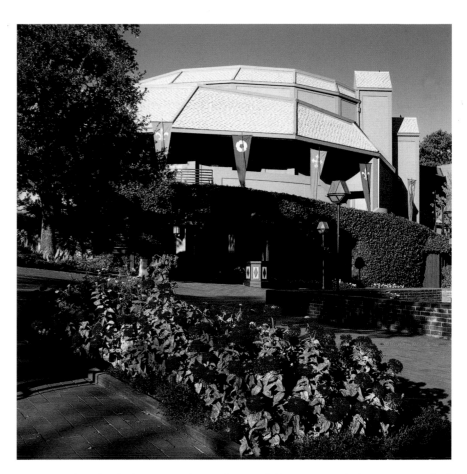

The Elizabethan Stagehouse, home of the Oregon Shakespeare Festival

The Winchester Inn (1886) a bed and breakfast in Ashland

Beautiful Toketee Falls in Douglas County

Opposite: Mount Thielson (9,182 ft) in the Umpqua National Forest

The end of the Lewis and Clark journey at Seaside on the north coast

The crashing surf of Cape Kiwanda at Pacific City

Beautiful Ecola State Park on the north coast

A typical Oregon sunset silhouettes the "Needles" at Cannon Beach

culminates at the highest point in the Coast Range (3,238 feet). If you prefer, you can travel to Saddle Mountain State Park by taking Highway 26 to the sign just past milepost 15. The seven-mile drive from Highway 26 to the base of Saddle Mountain provides a great view of the coast on clear days.

Tillamook Head Trail is a six-mile hike in and back. You can start either at Indian Beach in Ecola State Park, or at the entry south of Seaside. Local historians believe this was probably the route Lewis and Clark took when they came to Ecola Creek in 1806. Another lovely hike is the Neah-Kah-Nie Mountain trail that provides views of 30-mile stretches of the coast. A final recommendation is the Cape Falcon Trail which gives glimpses of the wonderful coastal rain forests.

Seaside and Cannon Beach are close sisters in beauty as well as in a plethora of activities. Haystack Rock is a much-photographed free-standing monolith that is a visual trademark of the Cannon Beach area. Jutting up 235 feet from the water near the beach, the rock is a natural investigative site for studying inter-tidal habitats and nesting birds. Members of the Haystack Rock Awareness Program instruct visitors on the wonders of this marine resource.

Ecola State Park marks the site where Lewis and Clark and Sacajawea ended their journey. Clark noted the site as a "butifull sand shore." His journey across Tillamook Head was prompted by his interest in purchasing a supply of whale meat from Indians who had a small village on Ecola Creek. On his visit he recorded that there was a whale's skeleton on the beach that was 105 feet long.

It was this site, too where one of the early settlers, a sailor named John Gerritse, hauled a cannon out of the ocean near Arch Cape. The cannon was determined to have come from the U.S. Survey Schooner Shark, which wrecked on Clatsop Spit just inside the mouth of the Columbia River in 1846. It is said that two other cannons were discovered at the same time and that when Gerritse went back to recover them they had again been buried by the shifting sands. In 1953 two cannons, constructed to resemble the originals, were placed at each entrance to the community of Cannon Beach.

South of Cannon Beach three striking headlands – Arch Cape, Cape Falcon, and Neahkahnie Mountain are showcased by Oswald West State Park. A short hike down the beach brings you to Smuggler's Cove, reputedly a pirate's haven in years gone by. You may want to set camp in the area so you can search for the 18th-century treasure chest that's said to be buried somewhere on Neahkahnie Mountain.

In Indian language, Tillamook means "land of many waters" – an apt description. Tillamook's lush grasses, nurtured by as much as 75 inches of rain a year, sustain the herds that compose Oregon's dairy industry. Much of the county's annual milk production of 25 million gallons is made into natural cheddar cheese at the Tillamook Cheese Factory just north of town. The factory attracts more than 800,000 visitors each year who stop in to buy souvenirs and have an ice-cream cone. Another great cheese stop is the Blue Heron Cheese Company, housed in a blue and white barn surrounded by pastures. Here, you can sample distinctive Brie and other cheeses, dips and Oregon wines while you browse the gift shop.

In addition to its agricultural importance, Tillamook is a major recreational center. Charter boats for crabbing and deep sea fishing are available and jetty, river, and surf fishing are popular. Clamming, beachcombing, hiking, hang gliding, scuba diving, and canoeing are among the many other offerings.

Leaving Tillamook, take the Three Capes Scenic Drive. This 40-mile loop serves as the gateway to some of the most diverse coastal scenery to be found in Oregon and offers a look, too, at the salt marshes and commercial oyster-shucking operations along Tillamook Bay. At the top of Cape Meares, a short hike leads to an abandoned lighthouse and the accompanying views of offshore islands that teem with sea birds and sea lions.

Drive a short distance further to Netarts Bay and you can feast upon grilled crab and blackberry pie.

A cluster of other little towns require just a short drive from Tillamook. Garibaldi is a deep sea port for charter and commercial fishing; Nehalem has a great little winery and park; Manzanita is a resort community; Wheeler hosts the annual Nehalem Bay canoe races; Rockaway Beach

Early morning glow at Yaquina Bay in Newport

Heceta Head Lighthouse, Devil's Elbow State Park, Lane County

Opposite: A spectacular view from Cascade Head on the central coast

features wide sandy beaches, fishing and swimming lakes, shopping and recreation; and Twin Rocks and Oceanside offer places to stay within easy distance of agate hunting.

You'll want to revive your kite-flying skills when you see the beaches at Lincoln City. Kites always dance in the wind over the beaches, but the best spectacle is in May and September when the town hosts a kite flying festival that's earned it the title of Kite Flying Capital of the World.

Lincoln City is an angler's paradise year round. Ocean charter fishing trips can be arranged out of Depoe Bay, or the Siletz River is a great spot for Chinook salmon, steelhead and trout. The Siletz Bay offers perch, crab and flounder. Devils' Lake has trout, perch, catfish, crappie and largemouth bass.

Lincoln City has a new billing as a shopper's Mecca. The Quality Factory Village houses discount stores for over 45 popular brand-name businesses.

The funky little town of Depoe Bay is billed as having the smallest harbor in the world. Highway 101 is the main street here, and nothing but a sea wall separates the town from angry Pacific storms. A rough winter storm can sometimes hurl the breakers right over the highway.

Gleneden Beach, just south of Siletz Bay, is home to the five-star resort, Salishan. Here, you'll be treated to excellent service, gourmet dining, an acclaimed wine list, oceanside golf, and what else? — shopping.

Also near Depoe Bay is a popular spot called Boiler Bay Wayside. The power of the ocean is evident both here and at the Spouting Horn, where seawater shoots skyward as it is forced through crevices in the basalt rock cliffs.

Long a favorite vacation spot, Newport and the nearby countryside have continued to blossom with activities that delight every age group. Whether you're on the fast track of life or seek to slow things down a little, there's plenty to draw from around here. The delightful ocean views, exciting winter storms and generally moderate temperatures add to the attraction.

Every kind of water-related activity can be had in this area. With the ocean on one side, and five major rivers draining into the area, the bigger problem would be deciding what not to do.

"Must do" activities in this area include stops at some of the community's notable learning centers and visitor attractions. The Oregon Coast Aquarium consistently is vistors' number one choice of places to see and it never disappoints. But don't forget some of the other attractions, because they are exceptional. Listed as one of the top 500 attractions in the country, the Marine Science Center on Yaquina Bay is the coastal research, teaching and marine facility for Oregon State University. The Science Center sponsors whale watching programs during the winter and has a good aquarium and museum. If sea creatures attract you, don't miss the Undersea Gardens. Here, a wonderful display of marine animals and plants is housed. Scuba diving shows are held regularly.

While in town, check out the Wax Works and Ripley's Believe It Or Not. Animated wax figures will take your breath away at the Wax Works and you'll hold it again when you see the displays of bizarre and unusual mysteries of nature and technology housed at Ripley's.

The Lincoln County Historical Society Museums, the Yaquina Art Center, and the Newport Performing Arts Center are all spots you won't want to miss, either.

For a visit back in time, tour the Yaquina Bay Lighthouse. The lighthouse was constructed in 1891 as a harbor entrance light for Yaquina Bay and is the only surviving example in Oregon of a lighthouse with a combined keeper's dwelling and light tower. The lighthouse is also the oldest existing building in Newport.

Nestled along the mouth of the Alsea River, Waldport is popular among salt and freshwater fishermen. The coastline on both sides of Alsea Bay varies from smooth sandy beaches to rugged rocky formations. Hiking, agate hunting, clamming, and crabbing are popular pursuits in many of the state parks in the area.

The small village of Yachats gathers its share of the anglers in Oregon. They arrive for the smelt season, which occurs every year between April and October. A perfect spot for the painting easel is Cape Perpetua, just south of town. Cape Perpetua is the highest point on the Oregon coast, and it offers a dramatic ocean view from its 800-foot headland.

A few miles down the road, just north of Florence, the Sea Lion Caves are home to hundreds of Stellar sea lions. Their cave home soars to the height of a twelve-story building and stretches

Morning beauty of Shore Acres Botanical Garden near Coos Bay

The rugged and beautiful cliffs at Shore Acres State Park

the length of a football field. It is a richly multi-hued geologic wonder that is among the largest and most beautiful caves in the world. The tour includes scenic pathways and an elevator that carries you 208 feet down into one of the largest sea caves in the world.

The city of Florence is, in itself, a delightful place to spend some time. Known as the City of Rhododendrons, the dramatic scenery of the area is enough to recommend it as a stopover. There are breathtaking views of rugged coastline, miles of magnificent beaches, and spectacular mountains of sand at the Oregon Dunes National Recreation Area. Florence's picturesque harbor, where fishing boats lie against a backdrop of the restored buildings of Florence's Old Town, is a delightful place.

Over 2,000 campsites are available, many near the ocean, while others are tucked away in the woods near creeks and freshwater lakes. Outdoor action is the main theme, for you can water ski, scuba dive, spear fish, jet ski, sailboat, sailboard, canoe, river raft, or jump into one of the great old-fashioned swimming holes. If that doesn't drain your energy, there's always the sand dunes and a buggy ride, or a romantic horseback ride along the beach.

The town of Coos Bay revolves its business around the bustling port that has become one of the busiest export stations for forest products in the world. Coos Bay and her neighboring town of North Bend offer visitors a glimpse of busy port city activities and so much more.

One of the most delightful attractions in the area is Shore Acres State Park. It features formal English gardens, a Japanese pond, and flowers that have been brought in from around the world. Here, the combination of the gardens, the rugged shoreline, the sandstone bluffs, and a covered observatory combine to create a photographer's paradise.

A natural wonder is the Oregon Dunes National Recreation Area. This area encompasses 32,000 acres of dunes, marshes and forestland stretching forty-one miles from North Bend to Florence.

Among the many other parks to visit, some particularly pleasant stops are Small Boat Basin, in Charleston; Sunset Bay State Park; Tenmile Lakes; and the South Slough National Estuarine Reserve. There are also numerous small delightful historical museums ranging from a logging museum to a newspaper museum. Don't forget the lighthouse tours!

Traveling south on Highway 101 you'll reach the coastal village of Bandon. Along this route you will see what many believe to be the most beautiful beach views in Oregon. Natural sea sculptures such as Elephant Rock, Table Rock, and Face Rock call out for use of a camera.

Lying within a coastal "banana belt," the Brooking Harbor and Port Orford areas offer much in addition to pleasant weather. The collection of craft stores, gift shops, galleries and charming restaurants that proliferate elsewhere along the Oregon Coast can be found here too. The towns are surrounded by deep forests, turquoise rivers and freshwater lakes, and you can find times when the beaches will be entirely your own. Over 300 species of birds make the area their home at various times of the year and wildflower enthusiasts will be spellbound – the climate allows for an almost year-round blooming season.

Near Brookings, the Azalea State Park, a botanical park noted as a favorite with bird watchers, blooms with azaleas from April through June. Loeb State Park is one spot where you can see the myrtlewood trees, and the Oregon Redwood Trail takes you along many lovely streams where canopies of huge redwood trees loom overhead and rhododendrons mark your passage.

The Oregon Coast, like the other areas of Oregon, has a charm of its own. Oregon's beauty is legendary and the state retains the ability with today's inhabitants and visitors to make them smile over the greatness of it all – just as the pioneers did before them.

Golden light of evening on the Oregon Dunes National Recreation Area, Coos County

Opposite: A beautiful sunset at Boardman State Park on the south coast

About The Photographer

The quiet dignity of Larry Geddis is a pleasant surprise in this day of super egos. And he goes about his chosen vocation–photography–in the same quiet, business-like way. But don't let the soft demeanor fool you, for here is a determined, athletic, energetic, and dedicated person who pursues his trade with a passion and an artistic eye, second to none.

Larry left his school teaching job in 1989 to follow his successful career in scenic photography. And successful he is, with two new books to his credit, Beautiful America's Oregon Coast and Beautiful America's Columbia River Gorge—plus three signature calendars with Beautiful America, Oregon, Columbia Gorge and Oregon Coast. His photos appear on note cards, in magazines and numerous other publications, including those of the Portland Chamber of Commerce, Portland/Oregon Visitors Association and the Oregon Tourism Division.

An avid backpacker, Larry has hiked repeatedly through the designated wilderness areas of Oregon, always searching for yet another beautiful landscape to photograph.

About the Author

"As a native Oregonian, I'm pleased to write about my state, but it is a daunting task to tell Oregon's story in one brief book – one book can't begin to tell of Oregon's wonders. One thing is certain. If you visit the state, you will fall in love with its beauty and its people."

Linda Stirling has over two decades of writing, advertising, marketing and public relations experience. She has been an advertising manager, a business editor, a director of sales and marketing, a newspaper manager, a freelance editor and writer, and has managed one publishing company and co-owned another. This is her seventh book for Beautiful America. In addition to her writing, she is currently Director of Marketing and Public Relations for the Hood To Coast Relay, the largest relay in the world.

Linda and her husband, Joe Grandy, reside just outside Portland, Oregon. She has five children and two grandchildren who all make the Northwest their home.

The absolute beauty of the south coast at Bandon Wayside State Park

Rear Cover: A deer at Wallowa Lake in northeast Oregon